ELEPHANTS
CLOSEUP

CLOSE UP

Dr. Carla Litchfield

wild dog

ELEPHANTS are the largest land animals on Earth. There are elephants that live in Africa, and elephants that live in Asia. African elephants are bigger than Asian elephants. All African elephants have tusks but only some male Asian elephants have tusks.

Though **ELEPHANTS** have thick, tough skin, their skin is very sensitive to the sun, and moms will often shade their young to prevent them from getting sunburnt.

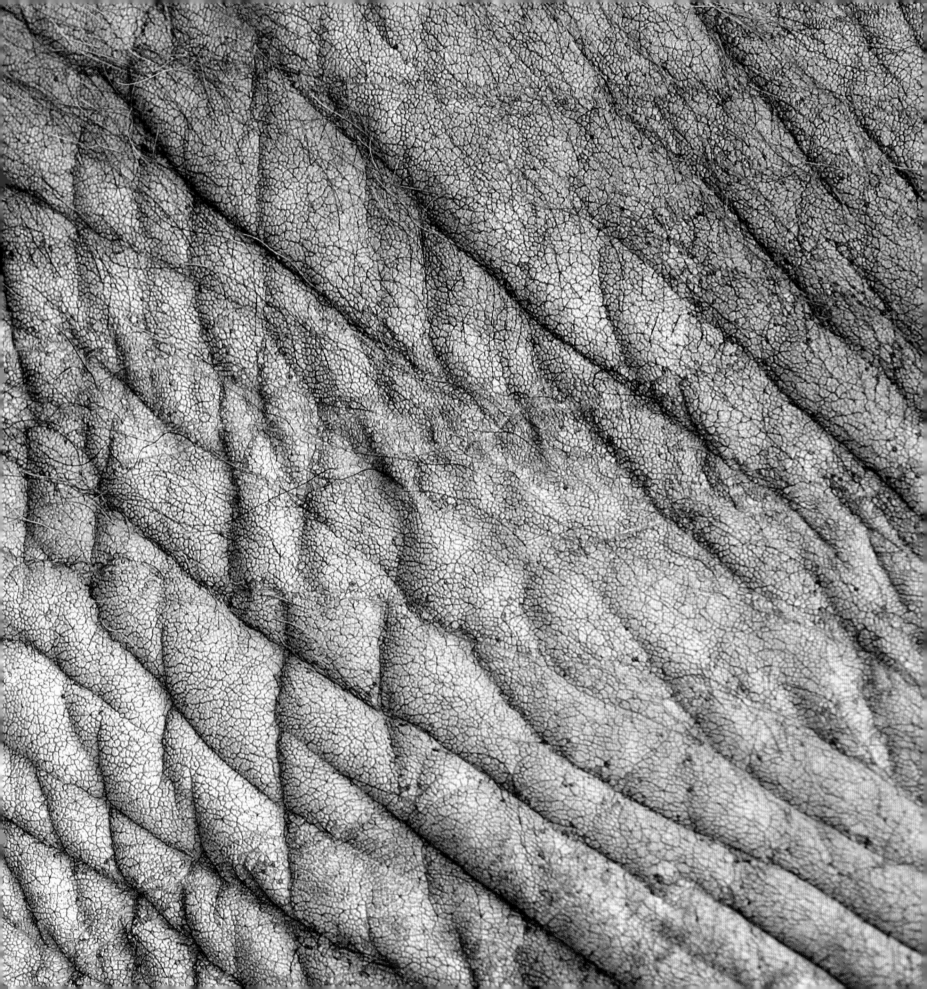

ELEPHANT tusks are used to dig for food, to move branches out of the way, and sometimes, as weapons when fighting with other elephants.

African ELEPHANT ears are about three times the size of Asian elephant ears.

An Asian elephant

ELEPHANT trunks are used for gathering food, drinking, washing, smelling, and communicating with other elephants. Trunks allow elephants to reach the tasty top branches that they love to eat.

ELEPHANTS have straight legs and large padded feet that help support their weight. Male African elephants can weigh up to 7 tons!

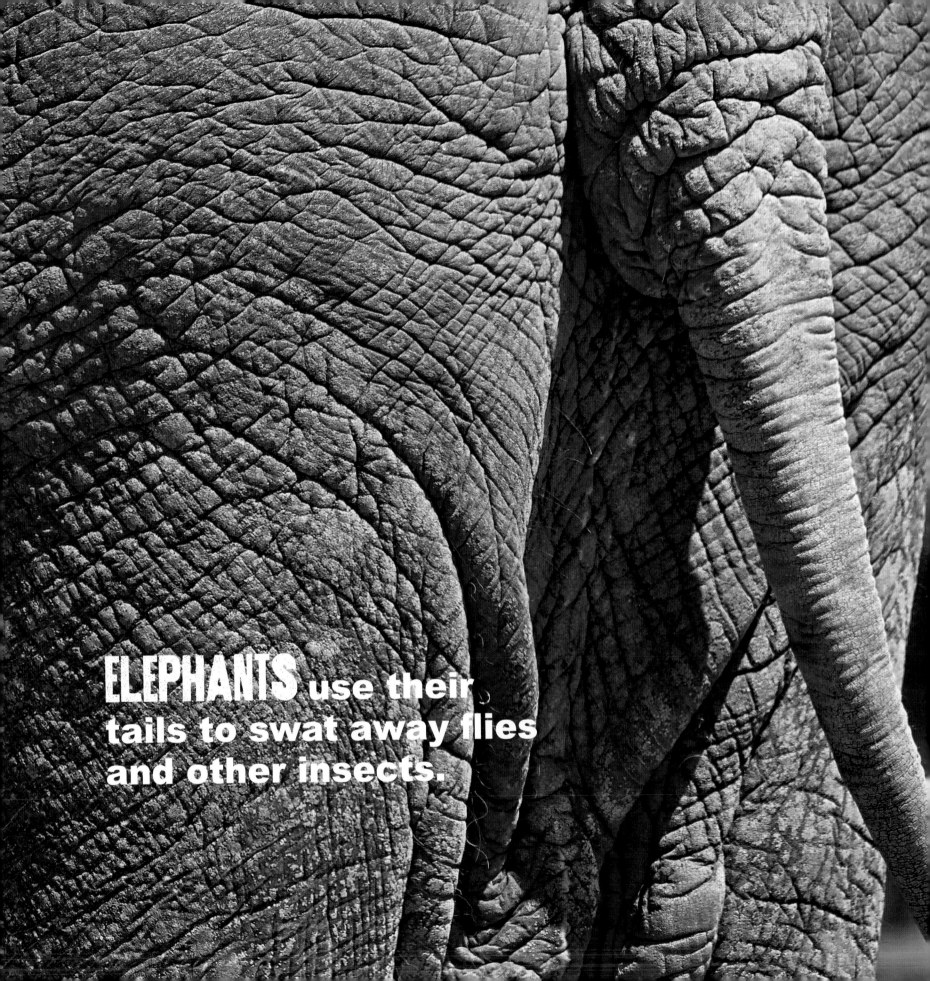

ELEPHANTS use their tails to swat away flies and other insects.

ELEPHANTS have quite poor eyesight, and they rely on their excellent sense of hearing and smell.

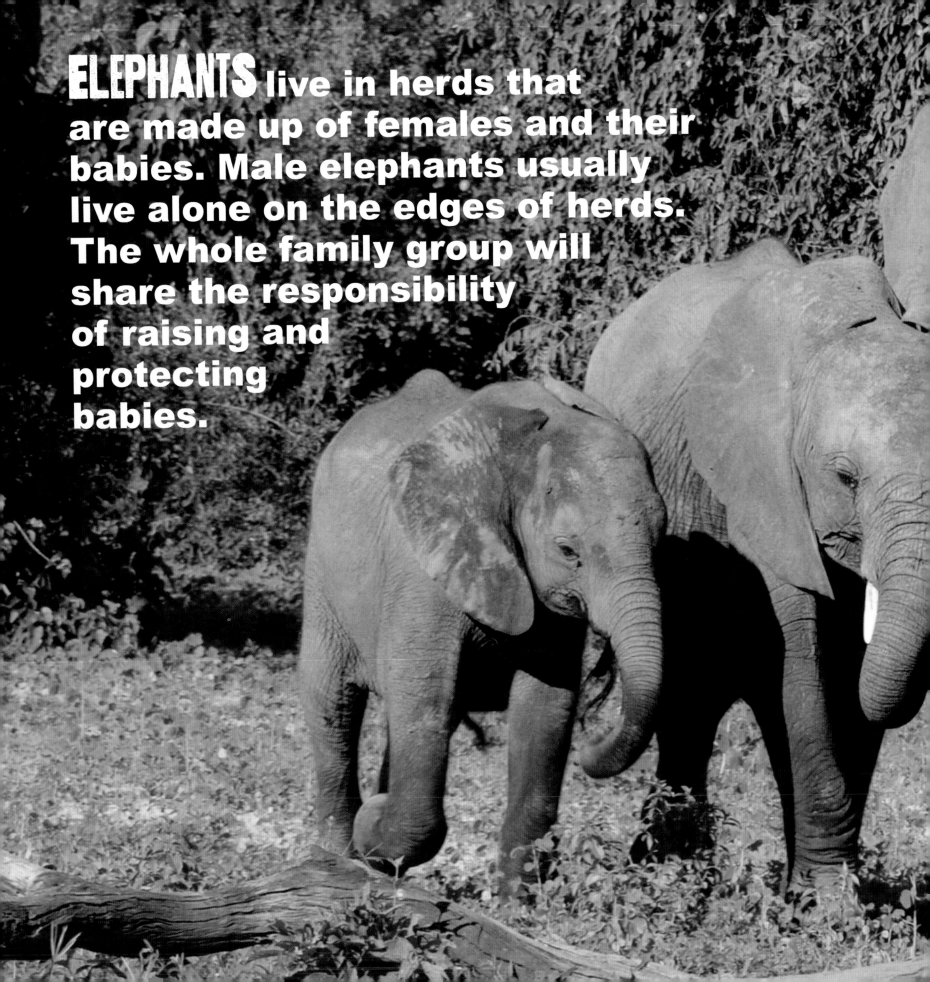

ELEPHANTS live in herds that are made up of females and their babies. Male elephants usually live alone on the edges of herds. The whole family group will share the responsibility of raising and protecting babies.

ELEPHANT newborns can weigh up to 220 pounds, and can drink up to 12 quarts of milk a day.

ELEPHANT babies are dependent on their moms and other females in the herd for up to five years after they are born.

ELEPHANT babies cannot use their trunks with any skill.

As they grow up, young elephants gradually learn how to pick up things with their trunks, how to drink, and lots more.

ELEPHANT adults can sleep standing up, but babies will nap lying down.

ELEPHANT babies are very social, and they love to play. Play is important, as baby elephants will learn lots of things about how to be a grown-up elephant this way.

First published in 2012 by

wild dog books

54A Alexandra Parade
Clifton Hill Vic 3068
Australia
+61 3 9419 9406
dog@wdog.com.au
www.wdog.com.au

Printed and bound in China by Everbest Printing Co Ltd

Distributed in the U.S.A. by
Scholastic Inc.
New York, NY 10012

ISBN: 978-1-74203-521-5 (pbk.)

5 4 3 2 1   12 13 14 15

PHOTO CREDITS:

All images courtesy of Shutterstock

GLOSSARY:

HERD: a group of animals that live, feed and travel together.
TRUNK: the long nose of an elephant.
TUSK: a very long tooth that sticks out of the mouth and is usually one of a pair.

GLOSSARY:

CANINES: long teeth used for biting and tearing.

GLANDS: an organ that releases chemicals.

HABITAT: the natural home or environment of an animal or plant.

PREDATOR: an animal that hunts and eats other animals.

PREY: an animal that is hunted or eaten by another animal.

BIG CATS love to play. Play is important for cubs to learn hunting behaviors. They can practice stalking and capturing playmates in safety.

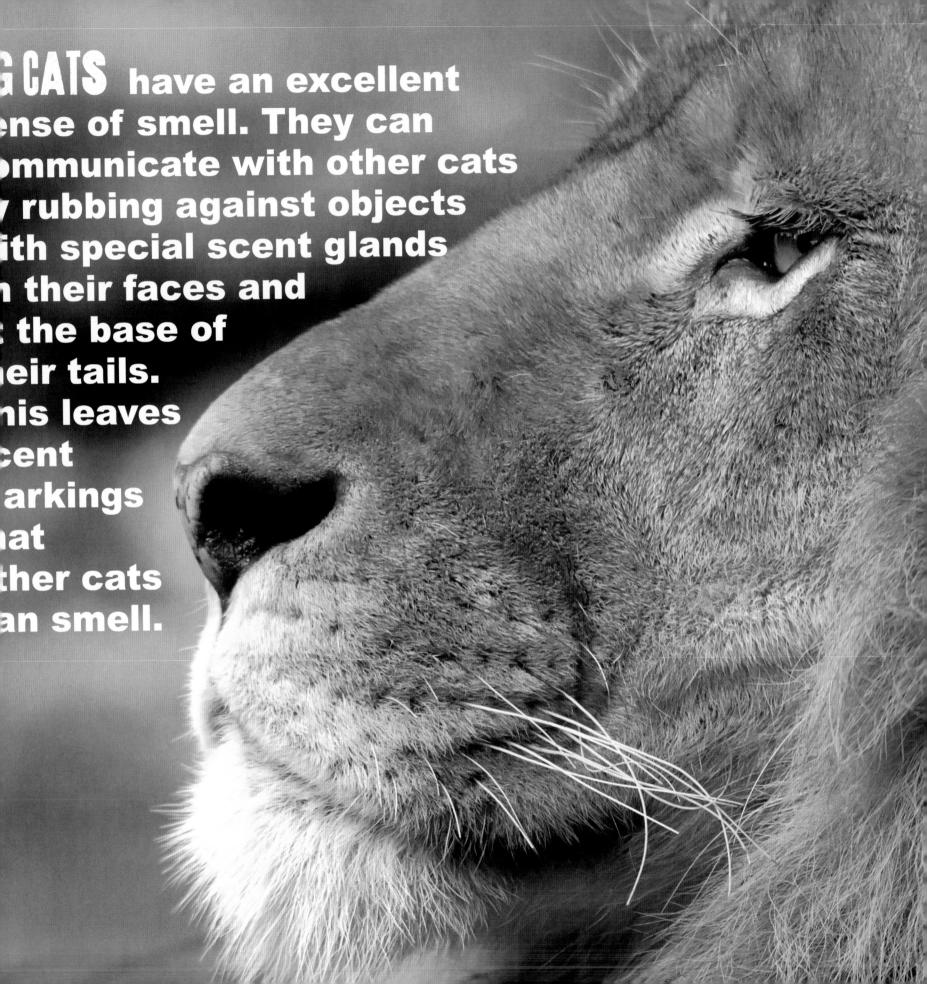

CATS have an excellent sense of smell. They can communicate with other cats by rubbing against objects with special scent glands on their faces and at the base of their tails. This leaves scent markings that other cats can smell.

BIG CATS all have very large canine teeth on the top and bottom of their mouths. Tigers and clouded leopards have the longest canines of all the big cats.

BIG CATS are excellent hunters. As with most predators, their eyes face forward, which enables them to see easily how close or far away something is.

COUGARS are found in the Americas, and are also known as mountain lions or pumas. While they are good hunters, they often have to compete for food with other large predators such as grizzly bears or wolves.

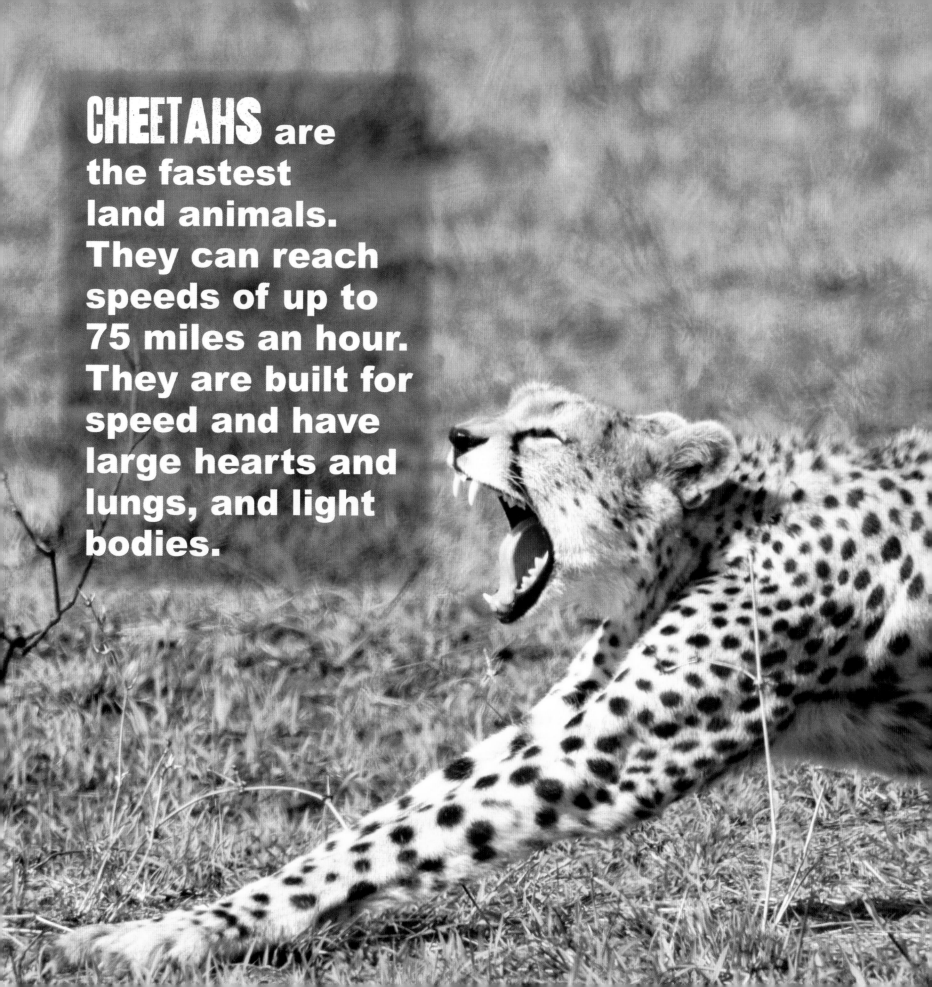

CHEETAHS are the fastest land animals. They can reach speeds of up to 75 miles an hour. They are built for speed and have large hearts and lungs, and light bodies.

SNOW LEOPARDS live in the high mountains of Central Asia. They have many special features that help them live in the snow, including wide paws for walking on snow, and long thick fur which keeps them warm.

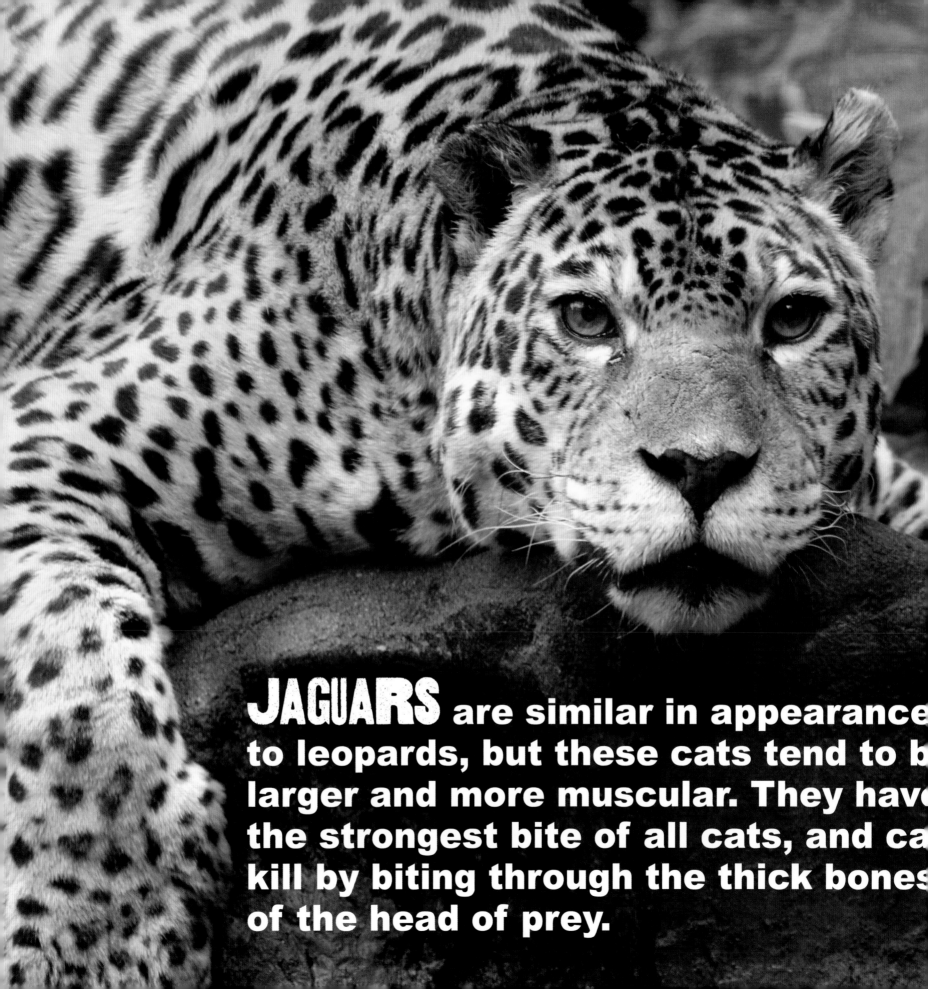

JAGUARS are similar in appearance to leopards, but these cats tend to b larger and more muscular. They have the strongest bite of all cats, and ca kill by biting through the thick bones of the head of prey.

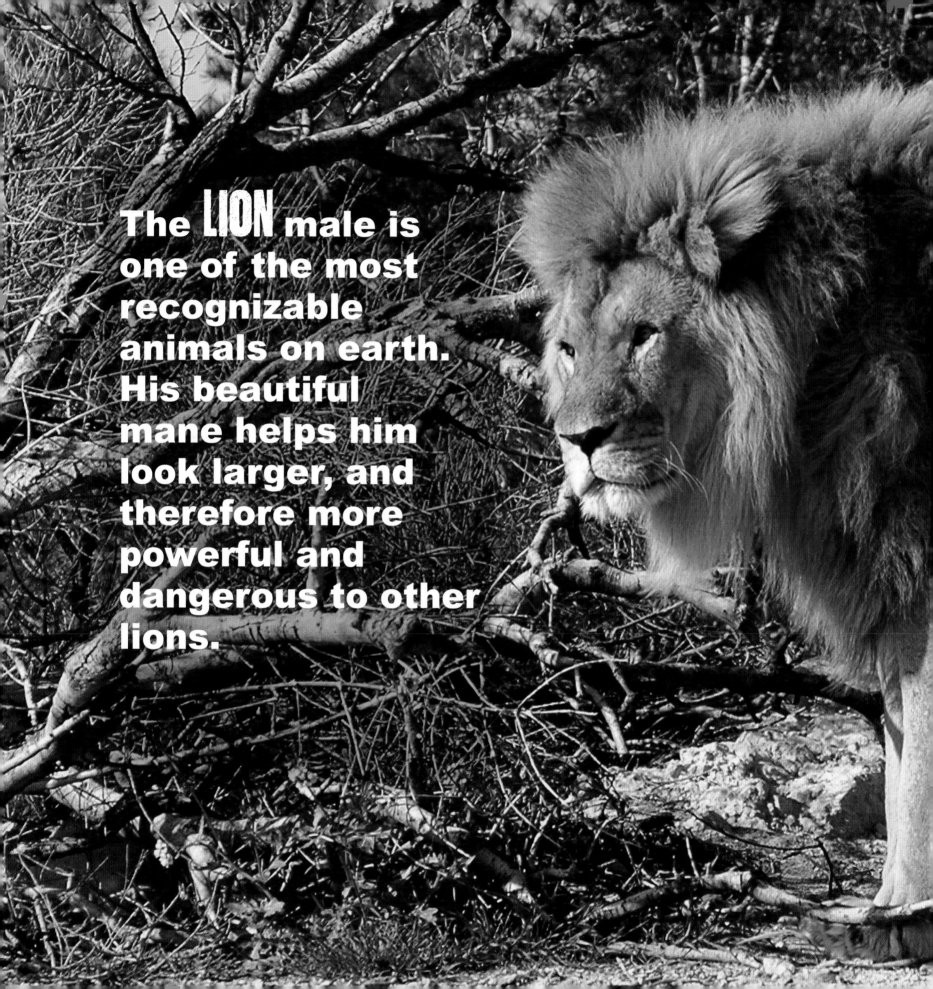

The LION male is one of the most recognizable animals on earth. His beautiful mane helps him look larger, and therefore more powerful and dangerous to other lions.

LIONS are the second largest cat on earth, and are the most social of all the big cats. They live in groups called prides, which are made up of females, cubs, and one or more males.

LEOPARDS have spotted coats, which makes them perfectly camouflaged in the grasslands, woodlands and forests where they live. They can creep to within a few feet of their prey.

The stripes on **TIGERS** allow them to blend in with the trees, grasses, or the shadows of the forest as they hunt prey. Every tiger's pattern of stripes is different, just as every human's fingerprint is.

Wild tigers are typically orange in color, with black or brown stripes. White tigers are usually only found in captivity.

TIGERS are the largest of the **BIG CATS**. Tigers can weigh over 650 pounds. They can survive in many different habitats, from icy Siberia to the warm jungles of Asia.

BIG CATS are the tiger, lion, jaguar, and leopard. These are the biggest cats in the world, and the only cats that are able to roar. Big cats can also include the other large members of the cat family, such as the cheetah, cougar, and snow leopard.

BIG CATS CLOSE UP

CLOSE UP

Dr. Carla Litchfield

wild dog